SIGHT UNSEEN

GLORIA KROEZE

CRC Publications
Grand Rapids, Michigan

Acknowledgments

The Scripture quotations in this publication are taken from the HOLY BIBLE, NEW INTERNATIONAL VERSION, © 1973, 1978, 1984, International Bible Society. Used by permission of Zondervan Bible Publishers.

Printed in the United States of America on recycled paper. ♻

1-800-333-8300 (US); 1-800-263-4252 (CAN)

Library of Congress Cataloging-in-Publication Data

Kroeze, Gloria.
    Sight unseen / Gloria Kroeze.
       p. cm.—(Acts 2 for small groups)
    ISBN 1-56212-227-4
    1. Bible. N.T. Hebrews X, 19-XII, 3—Study and teaching.
    2. Faith—Biblical teaching—Study and teaching. I. Title.
    II. Series.
    BS2775.5.K76 1996
    227'.87'007—DC20   96-33506
                                            CIP

10 9 8 7 6 5 4 3 2 1

CONTENTS

INTRODUCTION

"Now faith is being sure of what we hope for and certain of what we do not see" (Heb. 11:1). With this memorable definition, the writer of Hebrews begins his inspiring description of men and women of great faith.

Sight Unseen, a seven-session course for small groups, is a study of these heroes of faith. By their example, we are encouraged to look beyond the immediate, to believe—and act on—the promises of God, to persevere when the going gets tough, to run the race of faith with our eyes firmly fixed on Jesus. In this way we too can become certain of things we do not see. We too can live by faith.

Sight Unseen is part of the *Acts 2* program for small groups. That program is described in detail below.

WHAT ARE *ACTS 2* SMALL GROUPS?

Acts 2 small groups look and act much like the early church house groups portrayed in Acts 2:42-47. These groups were involved in teaching, fellowship, worship, prayer, enfolding, ministry, social time, and evangelism. All of these features are basic to the life of the church. The more these characteristics define a church's small groups, the more they will also define the larger congregation.

Acts 2 groups consist of three to fifteen people who are committed to meeting regularly together to support each other and explore some aspect of the Christian life. Six important features characterize an effective *Acts 2* small group.

MAJOR FEATURES OF *ACTS 2* SMALL GROUPS
BUILDING CHRISTIAN COMMUNITY

Acts 2 groups are more than study groups; study is only one of several important activities. The basic purpose of an *Acts 2* group is to build Christian community by developing meaningful relationships among group members. All of us long to be loved and cared for in an accepting and supportive environment. A good group fosters a level of trust and safety that makes intimacy possible. A healthy *Acts 2* group will meet relational needs by sharing the realities of life, praying with and for each other, ministering side by side, and having fun together.

FORMATTED MATERIALS

Each *Acts 2* meeting includes five main segments:

- Opening share time
- Bible discovery
- Reflection
- Prayer
- Planning for ministry

Groups that follow this format are likely to succeed. If these five elements are not deliberately built into each meeting, groups may shortchange themselves by inadvertently omitting, for example, silent reflection or ministry planning. The *Acts 2* materials provide a regular format that will ensure coverage of each element in all meetings.

TRAINED LEADERS

Ineffective leadership is the primary cause of failure in small groups. Qualified *Acts 2* leaders are trained, supported, and held accountable for what happens in their group.

A training workshop—"Small Groups that Build Up Christians and Churches"—is available (contact CRC Publications for details). After the training workshop and before starting their own *Acts 2* groups in their local church, leaders should experience an *Acts 2* group. This training will teach them the fundamentals of small group leadership by seeing and by doing.

In addition to training leaders, each church is urged to hold regular meetings for small group leaders. These meetings grant leaders the opportunity to enhance their leadership skills, learn from each other's insights and frustrations, report progress, and support each other. The leaders' group becomes, in essence, a support group for the leaders. Trained, supported small group leaders are much more likely to be effective.

GROWTH AND REPRODUCTION

Not many small groups have an outward focus. Small groups often become ingrown and self-serving, a holy huddle that shuts out the concerns of nonmembers. To break this pattern, a small group must deliberately reach out. We suggest placing an empty chair at all your meetings to remind you of the next person God will bring to the group. Group members can pray for and seek persons to fill that chair. In addition, the group may sponsor or attend social events to identify and connect with potential new members. *Acts 2* groups aspire to grow and reproduce a new daughter group every two to three years.

New additions should always be a group decision. Members need to seek the approval of the whole group before inviting someone. New persons who attend should always start on a trial basis. If they don't fit into the group, they should be encouraged to look for another group where they will be more comfortable.

When *Acts 2* groups form new groups, the leader selects two or three members, including an apprentice leader, to be the core of the new group. The group then commissions them to form the new group and sends them off with a blessing. If other members of the group want to join this new group, they are free to do so, if invited.

MINISTRY ORIENTATION

A small group of people who study the Bible are in a good position to begin doing what it says. *Acts 2* groups do ministry as well as talk about it.

All members should be active in one or more of the roles needed to maintain the group:

- Leader
- Assistant or apprentice leader
- Host or hostess
- Prayer leader
- Service project coordinator
- Outreach facilitator or social activity coordinator

In addition, all are encouraged to pray for persons who might join the group or those who simply need prayers. All members are also encouraged to become involved in planned group service projects.

LEADER-RECRUITED GROUPS

Assigning people to groups may be the simplest and easiest way to start a cluster of small groups, but training several leaders and sending them to find their own group members is usually more effective. When a few of the invitees have accepted, the leader seeks their input in further choices. The group grows gradually as potential members respond to specific invitations. Groups that form this way are much more likely to bond, since they have chosen each other. They will also continue inviting others.

A church using this approach is likely to have a higher percentage of people involved in small groups than those using other methods. First, people sometimes say no to small groups because they fear being placed with people they don't like. The personal leader-recruiting system gives them more control over those with whom they will be grouped. Second, many people who will not respond to a public solicitation will respond to a personal invitation; this is especially true if the invitation comes from someone they know.

COORDINATED BY A DIRECTOR

Every local church with a small group program should have a director or coordinator of small groups. The director should schedule and lead regular leaders' meetings. He or she should receive reports from the leaders and hold them accountable to the goals they have set. The director should also visit each of the small groups two or three times a year and give the leader an outsider's perspective on the group.

The director, as servant-leader, should build a relationship with each small group leader or leader couple in order to extend needed support and encouragement. He or she should be available to help them formulate goals and plans, identify and recruit apprentice leaders, and find new members. The director should also be familiar with the church's greeting and welcoming systems and should be able to channel the names of church visitors to small group leaders.

WHAT HAPPENS IN AN *ACTS 2* GROUP?

One *Acts 2* small group I attended went like this:

Guests began arriving about ten minutes early for the seven o'clock meeting. On their way to the family room, they helped themselves to beverages and snacks set out by the hostess. Every person who arrived was greeted cordially, and we chatted about everyday things.

At about 7:05, the leader started the meeting, although everyone had not yet arrived. He asked a group member to read the first of the opening share questions. Responses were lively and numerous.

Another couple arrived and was welcomed by the group. For their benefit, the leader explained where we were in the session. The group continued sharing, moving on to the second (and more personal) of the sharing questions.

Our leader explained that some of the things we had been talking about were also addressed in today's Bible study. Someone read the opening comments and the Scripture passage. The leader read the first question and invited responses. We spent about twenty-five minutes digging into the Bible passages, using the discovery questions provided and asking some of our own questions. Twice our leader referred us to the "Helpful Notes" provided in the lesson. The study ended with the leader's summary of the main ideas.

A brief reflection time came next. Everyone worked individually and in silence as we wrote our personal responses to the four reflection questions. We had a chance to think about our own relationship with God and to prepare for the question that preceded the prayer time: "How do I want the group to pray for me?"

Before we prayed together, most of us shared some joys and concerns. We mentioned needs in the lives of hurting persons we knew. Though some of us were a bit nervous about the prayer time, the leader put us at ease by starting us out with one-word prayers of praise. He began with "Father God, we praise you for . . . " and we completed the sentence by naming a dozen or more qualities of God. Next came "Father, we thank you for. . ." and we finished the sentence with short expressions of gratitude. Finally we said one- or two-sentence prayers of intercession. Someone remembered to pray for the person who would fill our empty chair. This was a comfortable and stimulating time.

The last thing we did was plan for ministry. We started by identifying three unchurched persons who would be on our prayer list. We added two singles who were fringe members of our church and a young couple who were just beginning to attend. We agreed that each of us would pray for each of these people a couple of times each week.

We made no progress on planning a social event, but we did decide to ask the pastor for a list of people attending the church's new member class. We also chose to take on one service project during the year. One couple agreed to lead this.

After the formal meeting, we took more refreshments and continued to visit with each other. Some group members left almost immediately. Two couples lingered for another half hour.

FUNDAMENTALS OF SMALL GROUP LIFE

FIVE BASIC FUNCTIONS

A good group will ordinarily include

A social/recreational time. Fun time is a natural and important part of the life of the group. Activities apart from the regular meetings develop stronger group relationships and especially benefit the children of the families involved.

Life-application Bible study. The questions in the Bible study section of each lesson will help you discover what the Bible says. The application element is particularly important. People tend to lose interest in abstract discussions that do not relate to their lives.

Meaningful prayer time. Everyone should have a chance to share joys and concerns and contribute to the prayer time. Not everyone is expected to pray out loud, but everyone should be allowed to do so. Don't be afraid of periods of silence—during these times, individuals may pray silently or simply bow before God in silence. The prayer time may also be a time for worship—simply focusing on God and rejoicing in his goodness.

Regular sharing opportunities. The Christian life is meant to be a shared life. The New Testament emphasizes that Christians come to know each other well enough to bear each other's burdens, teach and admonish one another, and even confess faults to each other. This will happen best in a small group if members are free to share with the group what life is really like for them. Of course, what is shared *must* be kept confidential.

Ministry opportunities. Every believer has at least one spiritual gift. A small group is a wonderful place to use that gift and to find support. Don't let your small group become another sit-and-soak experience—the church already has enough of those.

GROUP PATTERNS

The best place for a group to meet is in a familiar, informal setting. Around a kitchen table or a family room is ideal.

Groups that meet weekly will have the most impact, but meeting weekly may not be realistic. Most groups meet biweekly or twice a month. Groups that meet less frequently lose the continuity necessary for building relationships. Biweekly meetings can be a little longer than weekly meetings but should be kept under two hours.

Each group should set growth and ministry activity goals and keep a record of its progress in meeting the set goals. Some things simply will not happen unless plans are laid and progress is regularly reviewed. Groups should try to spin off a new small group every two to three years. (See "Group Goals Planning Sheet on page 59.)

LEADERSHIP RESPONSIBILITY

The leader's primary responsibility is to organize and lead the regular small group meeting. This means facilitating the involvement of people in sharing, prayer, and Bible study and working to keep a healthy balance between these various elements. A good balance of available time is as follows:

- About 25 percent on sharing. *Acts 2* material suggests sharing before the Bible study and before the prayer time.

- About 25 percent on prayer. Initially you will probably not spend this much time in prayer; as the group members come to know each other, however, this time will likely increase.

- About 40 percent on Bible study.

- About 10 percent on ministry planning.

The notes in the margin addressed to the leader are intended to help you involve members in the various activities.

Between meetings, leaders should pray regularly for group members and continue contact with group members. Pastoral care is the responsibility of the whole group, but the leader must see that it is done.

Every leader should also identify an apprentice leader. This person can assist in leadership functions and prepare to lead a new spin-off group.

Leaders should spend several hours preparing for each meeting. Be thoroughly familiar with the main theme, the Bible passages, and the directions in the material. Prepare for each question (for some, perhaps you'd rather substitute your own questions). Highlight key phrases or words for easy reference during the meeting. Develop extra questions that can help the group probe an area that needs attention. Prepare your heart as well as your thoughts. Above all, blanket the group and the time you will spend together with prayer, asking God to direct and protect you and to make himself known through his Word and Spirit.

COMMON PROBLEMS TO AVOID

The problems described below are common to small groups. Any of them can severely diminish a group's effectiveness or even kill it.

Shallow relationships. Sharing our ideas but not ourselves, praying for others while hiding our own pain, applying biblical truths generally but avoiding specific personal application—these behaviors will yield shallow relationships. An increasing amount of honesty and openness are necessary in order to develop deep and meaningful relationships.

Overly intellectual discussions. Dealing only with the intellectual dimensions hinders spiritual growth and the development of Christian community. Try to spend at least half of your group study time relating biblical truths to your daily lives.

Unused gifts. A small group is a perfect place to identify, confirm, and use spiritual gifts. Groups in which one or two persons take charge do not promote gift development. Leaders are encouraged to share responsibility so that everyone is involved and challenged to use his or her gifts.

Problem members. Compulsive talkers, tangent-chasers, judgmental persons, pity-seekers, or domineering individuals can ruin a group. For the good of the group, leaders must deal with problem members lovingly but firmly.

Lack of confidentiality. Few things will shut down personal sharing faster than breaches of confidentiality. Be sure to regularly review the ground rules for preserving confidentiality and deal quickly with any compromise of these standards.

Little meaningful prayer. Perfunctory or impersonal prayers, quick opening and closing prayers, and prayers that do not touch our real lives will stultify a group. Prayer is one place where people can really connect with each other.

Holy huddles. Groups that focus inwardly soon become cliques or holy huddles. An intimate, close-knit group is not a clique as long as it looks to the interests of others as well as its own. An exclusive small group that shuts out the cares and concerns of others has a problem.

GETTING STARTED

After appropriate training, leaders should list people they would like to have in their group. The list should include twice the number needed, because only half of those invited are likely to accept.

The next step is to prioritize the list and extend invitations to those on top of the list. Give invitations with full explanation; ask people simply to try the group. Their decision to join does not need to be final until they have experienced at least two meetings.

Those who accept the initial invitation may help choose additional group members. When six to eight persons have accepted the initial invitation, set a date, time, and place for the first meeting. I suggest making the first meeting a social evening at which people get acquainted and are informed about the purpose and format of the group. They may also be asked at this time what they would like to study. Be prepared, however, to make a suggestion rather than to leave this wide open. Most new groups will welcome the leader's recommendation of material to be used. Give people plenty of time to ask questions too.

VALUE TO THE CHURCH

Small groups are of great value to the church. They provide a good place to grow. They're like greenhouses, shutting out the cold and letting in the light necessary for growth.

Small groups also decentralize caregiving. Small group members who know each other's needs and have regular contact can minister to each other in a way that diminishes the need for attention by paid staff.

Furthermore, small groups create a natural path for evangelism, assimilation, and discipleship. Relationships draw people to Christ, bring them into the church, and help them mature. Relationships are the primary strength of the small group.

Starting and maintaining a good small group program is not a quick and easy task. It requires gifted people, solid training, and constant administrative attention. Above all, it requires the grace and power of God released through prayer.

Acts 2 groups reflect the realities of the Acts 2:42–47 experience in which early Christians "devoted themselves to the apostles' teaching and to the fellowship, to the breaking of bread and to prayer" and in which "believers . . . had everything in common . . . gave to anyone as he had need . . . ate together with glad and sincere hearts . . . [and] added to their number daily."

> *Alvin J. Vander Griend*
> *Former Minister of Evangelism Resources*
> *Christian Reformed Church Home Missions*

Session 1
WHAT IS FAITH?

OPENING SHARE TIME
10-15 minutes

Sharing is an important function of *Acts 2* small groups. Notice that the first share time question is usually general and the second is more specific and personal.

1. We say "seeing is believing." How is faith different from that? What are some things in which people tend to put their faith today?

2. What kinds of things test your faith or make you doubt?

Leader: Distribute books and briefly explain our topic for the next seven weeks. Then discuss the two opening questions.

BIBLE DISCOVERY TIME
20-30 minutes

Read Hebrews 10:19-23. We do not know who wrote Hebrews. Some say it was written by Paul, but the style and emphases are unlike those found in Paul's letters. And Hebrews 2:3 identifies the author as a second generation Christian who heard the gospel from witnesses, not an apostle like Paul who encountered the Lord face-to-face.

We do know that Hebrews was written to Jewish Christians by an inspired believer. These new Christians were experiencing persecution and were in real danger of falling back into Judaism or of making the Christian faith like their old religion. The purpose of Hebrews was to encourage them to hang on to their faith in the resurrected Christ. They could not fall back into the legalism and "dead works" they previously had practiced.

In Hebrews 10:19-23, we see that faith is a full assurance that is rooted in Jesus Christ and his saving work for us.

> [19]*Therefore, brothers, since we have confidence to enter the Most Holy Place by the blood of Jesus,* [20]*by a new and living way opened for us through the curtain, that is, his body,* [21]*and since we have a great priest over the house of God,* [22]*let us draw near to God with a sincere heart in full assurance of faith, having*

Ask one or two group members to read the introductory comments and the Bible passage. Lead the group in discussing the questions that follow the passage.

*our hearts sprinkled to cleanse us from a guilty con-
science and having our bodies washed with pure
water. [23]Let us hold unswervingly to the hope we pro-
fess, for he who promised is faithful.*

Helpful Notes

Leader: Today's passage
refers to some Old
Testament practices that
may be unfamiliar, so you
may want to ask someone to
read the Helpful Notes
aloud prior to discussing the
questions.

- *A new and living way.* Jesus has provided a new
  way for us to meet God. Previously, only the
  high priest could approach God—and only
  once a year when the priest entered the Holy of
  Holies. A curtain kept the rest of the faithful at a
  distance. Now, however, all believers can
  approach God with confidence.
- *The curtain, that is, his body.* Instead of the curtain through which the high priest entered the
  Holy of Holies, Jesus provides a new and living
  access to God through his sacrificial death.
  When Jesus died, the temple curtain was torn
  from top to bottom.
- *Bodies washed with pure water.* In the Old Testament, the priests needed to bathe before meeting God in the temple. In the New Testament,
  the water of baptism confirms God's promise
  that we belong to him.

When discussing question I,
you may want to consider
some of the things on which
our access to God is *not*
based.

1. On what is our confidence based when we approach
   God? Do you personally approach God's throne with
   this confidence?

2. Look at the conditions for drawing near to God listed
   in verse 22. Try restating these in your own words.

3. What, according to verse 23, is the basis of our hope?

Read Hebrews 10:35-39. These verses encourage us to
persevere in our faith.

> [35]*So do not throw away your confidence; it will be
> richly rewarded. [36]You need to persevere so that when
> you have done the will of God, you will receive what
> he has promised. [37]For in just a very little while,*
>
> > *"He who is coming will come and will not delay.*
> > [38]*But my righteous one will live by faith.*
> > *And if he shrinks back,*
> > *I will not be pleased with him."*
>
> [39]*But we are not of those who shrink back and are
> destroyed, but of those who believe and are saved.*

Helpful Notes

- *"He who is coming. . . ."* This passage is quoted from Habakkuk 2:3-4. The writer of Hebrews is using Habakkuk as an example of someone who also exhorted God's people to "hang in there" during a very tough time.

1. What hope does this passage give us to persevere in our faith?

2. What is the rich reward that we are promised?

Read Hebrews 11:1-3. The writer now wants to impress on his readers that it's normal for believers to endure hardships without seeing (as yet) what has been promised. This is the essence of faith.

> [1]Now faith is being sure of what we hope for and certain of what we do not see. [2]This is what the ancients were commended for.
>
> [3]By faith we understand that the universe was formed at God's command, so that what is seen was not made out of what was visible.

1. Try putting the definition of faith (verse 1) into your own words.

2. What hopes do you have of which you are "sure"?

3. The author of Hebrews cites our belief that God created the universe out of nothing as an example of "being certain of what we do not see." What other examples of this aspect of faith come to mind?

4. Is there a promise of God that you are hanging on to, that gives you hope?

Leader: You may want to compare the definition of faith in Hebrews 1:1 to the Heidelberg Catechism's definition in Q&A 21.

Maybe someone in the group has a personal story of faith they would be willing to share as a means of encouragement.

MAIN IDEAS

- Faith is the deep assurance that we can approach God with confidence because of Christ's redeeming work.

- Faith allows us to persevere in the face of trials.

- Faith gives us hope in a sure thing: the promises of a faithful God.

- Faith is the way by which we are certain of crucial unseen realities: God's existence and his work in our lives.

Ask someone to read Main Ideas and Good News. Give the group an opportunity to react to the statements and to add any statements they feel are needed.

GOOD NEWS

"Do not throw away your confidence; it will be richly rewarded" (Heb. 10:35).

REFLECTION TIME

7-10 minutes

Leader: Group members work individually during this time. Jot down your own personal responses to reflection questions. You may want to point out that this section and our prayers often include praise or thanksgiving, confession, requests or petitions for ourselves, and intercession for others.

Jot down your own reflections in response to the questions below.

1. What have I learned today for which I can praise and thank God? Are there specific promises of God for which I can give thanks?

2. Are there Christians I know whose faith is being tested by illness or other difficulties? Could the group pray for these persons today?

3. Is there anything in this area of faith and perseverance for which I (privately) need to ask God's forgiveness?

4. In what areas would I like my faith to grow?

PRAYER TIME

PREPARATION

5-10 minutes

As you are comfortable, share any answers or parts of answers from questions 1-4. Share especially insights that will help the group pray meaningfully with you and for you. If you have any additional prayer requests for yourself or others, please share them at this time.

Leader: Go around the circle, giving each person an opportunity to share his or her response to one or two of the reflection questions. Encourage members to mention ways in which you as a group can pray for them.

PRAYER

10-15 minutes

- Begin by reading Habakkuk 3:2, 17-19 (printed below). This is one of the strongest affirmations of faith in the Old Testament. It's a wonderful passage to memorize and to reflect on during the week; substitute your own circumstances for those mentioned in the text.

Read these guidelines aloud before praying, so that everyone knows the format. Initially you may spend considerably less than the allotted time in prayer, but as the group grows closer, the time may expand.

> *²LORD, I have heard of your fame;*
> *I stand in awe of your deeds, O LORD.*
> *Renew them in our day,*
> *in our time make them known;*
> *in wrath remember mercy . . .*
> *¹⁷Though the fig tree does not bud*
> *and there are no grapes on the vines,*
> *though the olive crop fails*
> *and the fields produce no food,*
> *though there are no sheep in the pen*
> *and no cattle in the stalls,*
> *¹⁸yet I will rejoice in the LORD,*
> *I will be joyful in God my Savior.*
> *¹⁹The Sovereign LORD is my strength;*
> *he makes my feet like the feet of a deer,*
> *he enables me to go on the heights.*

- After the reading, group members may offer brief prayers of praise and thanks. Give thanks for the gift of faith, for access to God's throne, for specific promises of God, for a faithful God.

- Close the prayer time by remembering specific requests and by asking that we grow in our faith.

- Please feel free to contribute more than once. Expect some times of silence. Use them to listen to the Spirit or to offer a silent prayer.

PLANNING FOR MINISTRY

Leader: Refer the group to Appendix A, Group Goals Planning Sheet.

Service or ministry is an important function of *Acts 2* small groups. This section will suggest some ways that your group can plan for ministry.

If your group is meeting for the first time, you'll want to establish some goals for your meetings. Discuss each goal and consider its value to your group and your church before you set the goal. Be sure the goals are something you can accomplish.

If your group has been meeting for some time, review the group's goals and make any necessary revisions or additions.

Session 2
BY FAITH, ABEL AND ENOCH

OPENING SHARE TIME

10-15 minutes

Hebrews 11, the chapter we will be studying in detail, lists Abel and Enoch as its first heroes of faith. Both act out their faith and enjoy God's acceptance because of it. This kind of faithful living can be described as having "walked with God" (Gen. 5:22).

Leader: At the end of today's session we'll be talking more about your personal walks with God, so your initial discussion needn't be lengthy.

1. Suppose you and a neighbor agree to take a daily walk. What things are necessary for you to walk together?

2. What is necessary for you and God to walk together? What helps make your walk with God good, productive, close?

BIBLE DISCOVERY TIME

20-30 minutes

Read Hebrews 11:4 and Genesis 4:2-8. The writer of Hebrews reaches way back into ancient times to find his first example of faith.

Ask one or two group members to read the introductory comments and the Bible passages. Lead the group in discussing the questions that follow the passages.

⁴By faith Abel offered God a better sacrifice than Cain did. By faith he was commended as a righteous man when God spoke well of his offerings. And by faith he still speaks, even though he is dead.
—Hebrews 11:4

²Now Abel kept flocks, and Cain worked the soil. ³In the course of time Cain brought some of the fruits of the soil as an offering to the LORD. ⁴But Abel brought fat portions from some of the firstborn of his flock. The LORD looked with favor on Abel and his offering, ⁵but on Cain and his offering he did not look with favor. So Cain was very angry, and his face was downcast.

⁶Then the Lord said to Cain, "Why are you angry? Why is your face downcast? ⁷If you do what is right, will you not be accepted? But if you do not do what is right, sin is crouching at your door; it desires to have you, but you must master it."

⁸Now Cain said to his brother Abel, "Let's go out to the field." And while they were in the field, Cain attacked his brother Abel and killed him.

—Genesis 4:2-8

Helpful Notes

Leader: Wait to read the Helpful Notes until after you have discussed question 1.

- *He was commended.* God was pleased with him.
- *By faith, Abel offered God a better sacrifice.* Why was Abel's sacrifice better? Clearly, Abel's offering was motivated by true faith. For that reason he brought to God the best that he had. Cain's offering was not accepted because his motivation was seriously flawed. This was evident in his sacrifice of only "some of the fruits of the soil." It is also evident in God's warning that "sin is lurking at the door." Hardly the products of a true faith.
- *The LORD looked with favor.* The text is silent on how God demonstrated his acceptance of Abel's sacrifice and his rejection of Cain's.

1. Why do you think God accepted Abel's sacrifice and not Cain's?

2. What sacrifices does God desire of us today?

3. What are some unacceptable offerings that people give to God today? What makes them unacceptable?

When discussing question 2, you may want someone to read Psalm 51:17 and Romans 12:1 aloud.

4. "By faith he still speaks, even though he is dead." What does this mean, as applied to Abel? In what ways can our faith "still speak," even after we die?

Read Hebrews 11:5-6 and Genesis 5:18-24. Like Abel, Enoch is "commended as one who pleased God."

⁵By faith Enoch was taken from this life, so that he did not experience death; he could not be found, because God had taken him away. For before he was taken, he was commended as one who pleased God. ⁶And without faith it is impossible to please God, because anyone who comes to him must believe that he exists and that he rewards those who earnestly seek him.

—Hebrews 11:5-6

¹⁸When Jared had lived 162 years, he became the father of Enoch. ¹⁹And after he became the father of Enoch, Jared lived 800 years and had other sons and daughters. ²⁰Altogether, Jared lived 962 years, and then he died.

²¹When Enoch had lived 65 years, he became the father of Methuselah. ²²And after he became the father of Methuselah, Enoch walked with God 300 years and had other sons and daughters. ²³Altogether, Enoch lived 365 years. ²⁴Enoch walked with God; then he was no more, because God took him away.

—*Genesis 5:18-24*

Helpful Notes

- *He was no more.* Elsewhere in Scripture, this expression is sometimes a euphemism for death, but not here.
- *Because God took him away.* God literally *took* Enoch so that he did not experience death. Hebrews confirms this fact.

1. What does it mean to "walk with God"?

2. Reread Hebrews 11:6. What did Abel and Enoch both believe? How did God reward them?

3. "Without faith it is impossible to please God." Would you describe faith as the central thing God requires of us? How does our faith relate to God's saving grace?

4. Where does faith come from? How do we go about obtaining it?

Leader: When discussing question 3, group members may want to read Ephesians 2:8-9.

5. Think of someone you know who is a faith-full person. Share with the group one way that this person's life or actions demonstrate his or her faith.

MAIN IDEAS

- There is absolutely nothing we can do that will please God—unless we have faith.

- By faith in Jesus Christ, through the grace of God, we can approach our Father in heaven.

- Faith is an attitude of the heart, a desire to earnestly seek God.

- Faith shows itself in acts of worship and service done out of love.

Ask someone to read Main Ideas and Good News. Give the group an opportunity to react to the statements and to add any statements they feel are needed.

GOOD NEWS

"He [God] rewards those who earnestly seek him" (Heb. 11:6).

REFLECTION TIME

7-10 minutes

Jot down your personal reflections, using the questions below.

1. What have I learned today for which I can thank and praise God? Are there people of faith who have inspired and encouraged my own faith?

Leader: Group members work individually during this time. Jot down your own personal responses to reflection questions.

2. Is there someone I know whose walk with God is very much a struggle at the moment? Would it be appropriate for the group to pray for this person?

3. How would I describe my own walk with God? Do I approach God in faith, with an obedient heart? Or do I find myself going through the motions, wanting to come to God on my own terms? Is there a prayer request related to my walk with God that I would be willing to share with the group?

PRAYER TIME

PREPARATION

5-10 minutes

As you are comfortable, share any answers or parts of answers from questions 1-3. If you have additional requests for yourself or others, please share these at this time.

PRAYER

10-15 minutes

The focus of the prayer requests can be our personal walk with God, though other concerns and joys should be mentioned too.

Spend this time ministering to each other through prayer.

You may want to conclude by having someone read Habakkuk 3:2, 17-19, a passage printed in session 1. Or, if you prefer, sing "When We Walk with the Lord" or another song of your choice.

PLANNING FOR MINISTRY

Service or ministry is an important function of *Acts 2* small groups. This section will suggest some ways that your group can plan for ministry.

Talk about putting an empty chair in your circle at your next meeting. The chair can remind group members of the next person God will bring into your group. Group members can pray for and actively seek persons to occupy that chair: a member of your church who is no longer active; a neighbor, colleague, friend, or family member who doesn't belong to any church; or anyone else you feel would benefit from joining a small group.

Discuss other ideas that group members have for ministry. Ministry can be done together or individually.

One idea for individual ministry this week: write a note of thanks to someone who has inspired or encouraged you on your faith journey.

Leader: Our personal walk with God is a topic that demands a lot of intimacy and trust from group members. Some may not be ready for this or may simply prefer not to participate. Assure them that this is okay, and share your own feelings as openly as you can.

Try to make this an open time, being sensitive to different levels of comfort in praying. For variation, you may want to try a "candle prayer." Pass a lighted candle from member to member. As one person holds the candle, other group members offer prayers for that person. Prayers are based on what was shared during the preparation time.

Discuss the "empty chair" strategy with your group. This approach implies a deliberate outward focus and desire to grow. Is the group willing to commit to this?

Session 3
BY FAITH, NOAH

OPENING SHARE TIME

10-15 minutes

Noah is the next hero of faith mentioned in Hebrews 11. The writer of Hebrews commends him for showing faith when warned about "things not yet seen."

1. Everyday life demands a certain amount of faith, of accepting things "sight unseen," of hoping for things we cannot see. For instance, we order a book from a publisher's catalog and fully expect it to arrive in our mailbox. Think of some similar examples of things we tend to accept "by faith."

2. Have you ever taken a step of faith that left you vulnerable and "at risk" in some way? If so, please share your experience with the group.

Leader: Here's an alternative for question 2: What contemporary person do you admire for showing great faith? Why?

BIBLE DISCOVERY TIME

20-30 minutes

Read Hebrews 11:7 and Genesis 6:9-22. Noah demonstrates what we learned earlier about the definition of faith—being certain of what we do not see. Building a big boat in the driveway in a dry, landlocked area makes no sense *unless* you know what nobody can yet see—the flood's a-comin'!

Ask someone in your group to read the introductory comments. For the Scripture readings from Genesis, you may want to have one person read the lines that God speaks and another person read the narration.

> *⁷By faith Noah, when warned about things not yet seen, in holy fear built an ark to save his family. By his faith he condemned the world and became heir of the righteousness that comes by faith.*
> *—Hebrews 11:7*

> *⁹This is the account of Noah.*
>
> *Noah was a righteous man, blameless among the people of his time, and he walked with God. ¹⁰Noah had three sons: Shem, Ham and Japheth.*
>
> *¹¹Now the earth was corrupt in God's sight and was full of violence. ¹²God saw how corrupt the earth had become, for all the people on earth had corrupted their ways. ¹³So God said to Noah, "I am going to put*

25

an end to all people, for the earth is filled with violence because of them. I am surely going to destroy both them and the earth. ¹⁴So make yourself an ark of cypress wood; make rooms in it and coat it with pitch inside and out. ¹⁵This is how you are to build it: The ark is to be 450 feet long, 75 feet wide and 45 feet high. ¹⁶Make a roof for it and finish the ark to within 18 inches of the top. Put a door in the side of the ark and make lower, middle and upper decks. ¹⁷I am going to bring floodwaters on the earth to destroy all life under the heavens, every creature that has breath of life in it. Everything on earth will perish. ¹⁸But I will establish my covenant with you, and you will enter the ark—you and your sons and your wife and your sons' wives with you. ¹⁹You are to bring into the ark two of all living creatures, male and female, to keep them alive with you. ²⁰Two of every kind of bird, of every kind of animal and of every kind of creature that moves along the ground will come to you to be kept alive. ²¹You are to take every kind of food that is to be eaten and store it away as food for you and for them."*

²²Noah did everything just as God commanded him.
—Genesis 6:9-22

Helpful Notes

Leader: Refer to the Helpful Notes when they pertain to your discussion. A group member may read them aloud.

- *Blameless.* A term used most often to describe sacrificial animals, which had to be unblemished.
- *Condemned the world.* By pointing out the unbelief of the world around him, Noah made people aware of and responsible for their wrongdoing.
- *Walked with God.* Only Enoch had a similarly intimate relationship with Yahweh. Even Abraham, Isaac, and Israel's righteous kings did not get that close; the Scriptures say they walked "before God."
- *Filled with violence.* This phrase, which is repeated in this passage, shows that God had ample reason for sending the flood.
- *450 feet long.* By conservative estimate, the ark was one-and-a-half times the length of a football field, more than four stories high, and had

a volume within the decks of 1.3 million cubic feet.

- *Covenant.* Covenant refers to a binding agreement that is graciously initiated by the greater party and to which both parties are bound.
- *Did everything just as God commanded him.* Noah spent more than a hundred years being obedient to this one command of God. This crucial refrain appears several times in the story.

1. Noah had to accept, "sight unseen," that a flood was coming. What else must have required a good deal of faith from him?

2. Noah showed his remarkable faith by complete obedience. The text mentions nothing of what this obedience may have cost him. What may have been some of the pressures Noah faced in living out his obedience among people who knew him so well? Do we face similar pressures?

3. Why do you think Noah chose to obey God rather than cave into the pressures he must have faced?

4. When do you find obedience to God most difficult?

5. Do you think that when God looks at our world today he finds it as violent and evil as the world before the flood? If so, what keeps God from putting an end to things, here and now?

Read Genesis 7:1-10; 8:1; 9:8-11. Noah has taken the leap of faith necessary to build the ark. He has been obedient. Now God acts to save Noah and his family—and to bring judgment on a sinful world.

> [1]The LORD then said to Noah, "Go into the ark, you and your whole family, because I have found you righteous in this generation. [2]Take with you seven of every kind of clean animal, a male and its mate, and two of every kind of unclean animal, a male and its mate, [3]and also seven of every kind of bird, male and female, to keep their various kinds alive throughout the earth. [4]Seven days from now I will send rain on the earth for forty days and forty nights, and I will wipe from the face of the earth every living creature I have made."
>
> [5]And Noah did all that the LORD commanded him. Noah was six hundred years old when the flood-

waters came on the earth. *And Noah and his sons and his wife and his sons' wives entered the ark to escape the waters of the flood. *Pairs of clean and unclean animals, of birds and of all creatures that move along the ground, *male and female, came to Noah and entered the ark, as God had commanded Noah. *And after the seven days the floodwaters came on the earth.

—Genesis 7:1-10

*But God remembered Noah and all the wild animals and the livestock that were with him in the ark, and he sent a wind over the earth, and the waters receded.

—Genesis 8:1

*Then God said to Noah and to his sons with him: *"I now establish my covenant with you and with your descendants after you *and with every living creature that was with you—the birds, the livestock and all the wild animals, all those that came out of the ark with you—every living creature on earth. *I establish my covenant with you: Never again will all life be cut off by the waters of a flood; never again will there be a flood to destroy the earth."

—Genesis 9:8-11

Helpful Notes

- *God remembered Noah.* This is the heart of the story, the turning point from the complete destruction of the old creation to the beginning of a renewed one. The word "remembered" goes far beyond mere "recall"; when God "remembers" people in Scripture, he looks on them with compassion and love.

1. Once the rain began to fall, Noah's faith was validated. But imagine riding out a flood for more than a year, cooped up in a floating zoo. How do you suppose Noah's faith was further tested during that time?

2. What can we learn from the example of Noah?

3. What does the story of Noah and the flood teach us about God?

Leader: When discussing question 4, you may want to read Matthew 24:36-42.

4. How do you think the second judgment of God will be similar to the first judgment? How will it be different?

MAIN IDEAS

Leader: Ask someone to read Main Ideas and Good News aloud.

- God declares us "righteous" because of our faith in his promises.

- Our faith ties us to God in covenant obedience.

- What we cannot see must make us live in obedience until God fulfills his promises.

GOOD NEWS

"He [Jesus] became the source of eternal salvation for all who obey him" (Heb. 5:9).

REFLECTION TIME

7-10 minutes

Jot down your personal reflections in response to the questions below.

Group members work individually during this time. Jot down your own personal responses to reflection questions. You may want to point out that these personal, written reflections can continue to guide our prayers at home during the week ahead.

1. What has Noah's story shown me about God for which I can thank and praise him?

2. When I think about my own calling, my own place in life, am I living in faithful obedience? Do I offer excuses? Do I tend to complain too much? Is there anything for which I need to (privately) ask God's forgiveness?

3. Is God calling me to build an "ark" of some kind, to do something for him that will challenge and strengthen my faith? If not, should I ask God to make me open to such a venture?

4. How would I like others in the group to pray for me today? Are there others I need to ask the group to remember in prayer?

PRAYER TIME

PREPARATION

5-10 minutes

Leader: Go around the circle, giving each person an opportunity to share his or her response to one or two of the reflection questions. Encourage members to mention ways in which you as a group can pray for them.

As you are comfortable, share any answers or parts of answers from questions 1-4. Share especially insights that will help the group pray meaningfully with you and for you.

PRAYER

10-15 minutes

Ask a group member to read these guidelines before your prayer time begins. You may want to encourage your group members to jot down the personal needs of other group members as a prayer reminder throughout the week.

Begin your prayer time by praising God for the insights you have gained into his character through this session.

Move into a time of silence during which members can pray individually for forgiveness or for personal needs.

Continue by praying for any needs mentioned earlier.

You may want to close by singing (or reading in unison) the words of an old hymn, "If You But Trust in God to Guide You" (*Psalter Hymnal,* 446).

> *If you but trust in God to guide you*
> *and place your confidence in him,*
> *you'll find him always there beside you*
> *to give you hope and strength within;*
> *for those who trust God's changeless love,*
> *build on the rock that will not move.*
>
> *Sing, pray, and keep his ways unswerving,*
> *offer your service faithfully, and trust his word;*
> *though undeserving, you'll find his promise true to be.*
> *God never will forsake in need*
> *the soul that trusts in him indeed.*
>
> —Greg Newmark, 1641

As an alternative to the hymn, you may want to return to Habakkuk 3:2, 17-19.

PLANNING FOR MINISTRY

Today's session has focused on an amazing venture of faith. Is God calling your group to do something in faith for him? Praying faithfully for new members would be such a calling. So would a group service project, done in good faith that God will bless your efforts.

For an individual ministry project this week, consider our earlier question about building an "ark" (see "Reflection Time" question 3). Is there a venture of faith that God is calling you as an individual to undertake? Make it a matter of prayer this week. Consider sharing your thoughts and plans with another group member.

Leader: If your group is thinking about a service project, consult the deacons of your congregation. There may be existing needs that the group can help meet.

Session 4
BY FAITH, ABRAHAM AND SARAH

OPENING SHARE TIME

10-15 minutes

The list of ancients who lived by faith continues with Abraham and Sarah. In today's session we'll see how God put their faith to the test. Use the questions below to reflect a bit on this idea of "testing."

1. Why does a teacher give a test?

2. All of us face times in our lives when our faith in God is tested. If you feel comfortable doing so, please describe such a time in your own life.

Leader: Here's an alternative for question 2: When was the last time you took a test or exam of some kind, a really big one? How did it make you feel? How did you do?

BIBLE DISCOVERY TIME

20-30 minutes

Read Hebrews 11:8-10. We are now introduced to a married couple whose lives were characterized by remarkable faith. Abraham and Sarah were "sure of what they hoped for and certain of what they did not see." The writer of Hebrews describes three distinct ways in which their faith was put to the test. The first test came in the form of an immigration to Canaan.

> *⁸By faith Abraham, when called to go to a place he would later receive as his inheritance, obeyed and went, even though he did not know where he was going. ⁹By faith he made his home in the promised land like a stranger in a foreign country; he lived in tents, as did Isaac and Jacob, who were heirs with him of the same promise. ¹⁰For he was looking forward to the city with foundations, whose architect and builder is God.*

Helpful Notes
- *Faith . . . called . . . obeyed . . . went.* Once again, faith and obedience go hand in hand.
- *The city with foundations.* As a person of faith, Abraham looked for the definitive, permanent home that only God can provide. This kind of

For each of our four Scripture selections today, ask someone to read the introductory comments and the Scripture passage. Then discuss the questions that follow the passages.

Refer to the Helpful Notes when they pertain to your discussion. A group member may read them aloud.

permanent home—with God-established foundations—must have been especially appealing to people who spent their entire lives in tents.

1. Moving is always a lot of work, a big deal. What would have made it especially difficult for Abraham and Sarah? What do you think might have been going through Sarah's mind?

Leader: When discussing question 1, note that Genesis doesn't give us a clue about Sarah's attitude. But 1 Peter 3:6 does. You may want to check it out.

2. What do you think it meant for Abraham to live "like a stranger in a foreign country"? What does it mean for us?

3. Why did Sarah and Abraham do this? What motivated their faith? What motivates our faith?

Read Hebrews 11:11-12. The second test Sarah and Abraham faced was the long wait for the child God promised them. Through this child, God said, they would become the progenitors of a great nation.

> *[11]By faith Abraham, even though he was past age— and Sarah herself was barren—was enabled to become a father because he considered him faithful who had made the promise. [12]And so from this one man, and he as good as dead, came descendants as numerous as the stars in the sky and as countless as the sand on the seashore.*

Ask someone to read Genesis 17:17 for Abraham's reaction and Genesis 18:10-12 for Sarah's. Do these lapses of faith strengthen or weaken the commendation they receive in Hebrews 11?

1. Desperately wanting children but being unable to have them is a fearsome test of faith for anyone. What made it even more so for Sarah and Abraham? How do you think they felt during this time of waiting?

2. What promises of God are we waiting to see fulfilled? Does the waiting test our faith?

3. Despite their doubts, Abraham and Sarah believed in God's promise of a child. And God fulfilled that promise in the birth of Isaac, whose name means "he laughs." Share one promise of God that you have seen fulfilled in your life.

Read Hebrews 11:13-16. The writer of Hebrews wants to make sure we don't miss his point, so he takes us on a little detour from the main story.

> *[13]All these people were still living by faith when they died. They did not receive the things promised; they only saw them and welcomed them from a distance. And they admitted that they were aliens and*

strangers on earth. ¹⁴People who say such things show that they are looking for a country of their own. ¹⁵If they had been thinking of the country they had left, they would have had opportunity to return. ¹⁶Instead, they were longing for a better country—a heavenly one. Therefore God is not ashamed to be called their God, for he has prepared a city for them.

Helpful Notes

- *Aliens and strangers on earth.* The faithful lived as resident aliens on earth, longing for a "heavenly country." It is difficult for us to imagine the danger, difficulty, and loneliness of living like that, especially for an entire lifetime.
- *Has prepared a city for them.* The world may see the faithful as misfits and vagabonds, but God is not ashamed of them. He sees them as they shall one day be—as proud possessors of a heavenly city.

1. In what sense did Abraham and Sarah "not receive the things promised"?

2. How would this passage have encouraged the readers of Hebrews? Do you find it encouraging?

3. How would you describe the focus of the lives of the faithful described here? Is that still our focus today?

Read Hebrews 11:17-19. The detour is over and the writer returns to the main story, this time describing the third and most difficult test Abraham faced.

> *¹⁷By faith Abraham, when God tested him, offered Isaac as a sacrifice. He who had received the promises was about to sacrifice his one and only son, ¹⁸even though God had said to him, "It is through Isaac that your offspring will be reckoned." ¹⁹Abraham reasoned that God could raise the dead, and figuratively speaking, he did receive Isaac back from death.*

Helpful Notes

- *God tested him.* In the original Greek, "tested" means to test, to tempt, to put on trial. It's the same word used in James 1:13, which says (in the NIV) that God does not tempt anyone. The passages appear to conflict. But in James, the context of tempting is that of evil forces tripping us up. God never tests us for that reason.
- *Abraham reasoned.* Some have argued that reasoning is the enemy of faith. But if founded on

Leader: There are lots of questions in this session. Keep things moving along, skipping an occasional question if necessary.

faith, it can help us greatly. Abraham was quite right: God can and will find a way, even if it means raising people up from the dead. We hear echoes here of the trial God put himself through, a trial that cost him the life of his own dear Son, whom he actually raised from the dead.

Leader: If time permits, you may want to read part of Genesis 22:1-19, which describes this test of faith.

1. Imagine yourself as Abraham, walking up the mountain with Isaac, his beloved son whom God had told him to sacrifice. What would your feelings be? What could possibly get you through such an unthinkable ordeal?

2. Why do you think God pushed Abraham to this outer limit of faith? Why does God test us?

MAIN IDEAS

For variety, have group members sum up the key insights they gained from today's scripture.

- Faith calls us to believe in the promises of God and to willingly obey.

- We need to patiently trust in God's faithfulness to bring about what we may never realize in our lifetimes.

- God's tests us to temper, harden, and strengthen our dependency on him, never to cause us to fall into sin.

GOOD NEWS

"God is not ashamed to be called their [our] God; for he has prepared a city for them [us]" (Heb. 11:16).

REFLECTION TIME

7-10 minutes

Today's reflection time has a single focus: writing a prayer concerning an area of our lives where God is testing us. The prayer should be one that group members are willing to share with one other person.

Please think about the story of Abraham and Sarah. Reflect on this quote from Jim Elliot, who was martyred for his faith: "He is no fool who gives what he cannot keep to gain what he cannot lose" (*The Shadow of the Almighty*, Elisabeth Elliot).

With these things in mind, think about an area of your life where God is testing your faith. Then write out a prayer request related to this testing.

PRAYER TIME

PREPARATION

5-10 minutes

Please work through today's prayer time with a partner. As you are comfortable, share part or all of your written prayer with your partner.

After sharing, move right into praying for each other.

PRAYER

5-10 minutes

Partners may pray aloud for each other, based on their conversation during the preparation time.

After your prayer time, join together in a single large group. Close by singing or saying these stanzas of "Amazing Grace":

The Lord has promised good to me,
his word my hope secures;
he will my shield and portion be
as long as life endures.

Through many dangers, toils, and snares
I have already come;
'tis grace hath brought me safe thus far,
and grace will lead me home.

—John Newton, 1779

Leader: The partnership approach is for variation; it will also help each person become involved. Encourage group members to choose someone other than their spouse for their prayer partner. It's okay to have some groups of three. Include yourself in one of the groups.

Note the reduced time for prayer this week. After the partners have prayed for each other (about five minutes), call the group back together.

As an alternative to the hymn, you may want to return once more to Habakkuk 3:2, 17-19.

PLANNING FOR MINISTRY

Praying for each other during the week is a "ministry" in
every sense of the word. If you did the prayer partner
activity described above, why not continue praying for
each other each day this week?

Session 5
BY FAITH, MOSES

OPENING SHARE TIME

10-15 minutes

Moses, our next "hero of faith," is commended for making some very difficult choices, choices that carried enormous consequences.

1. Some say our high tech society offers us too many choices. Do you sometimes feel that way? If so, when? If not, why not?

2. Describe a choice you made that affected your life in a significant way, for better or worse.

Leader: A lighter alternative for one of the questions might be, "Describe a choice you made that resulted in unexpected and/or humorous consequences."

BIBLE DISCOVERY TIME

20-30 minutes

Read Hebrews 11:23. The writer of Hebrews does not soft-pedal what the consequences of our faith can be. From the very beginning of the story of Moses, we immediately sense the dangers of faith.

> *²³By faith Moses' parents hid him for three months after he was born, because they saw he was no ordinary child, and they were not afraid of the King's edict.*

For each of today's selections, ask one or two group members to read the introductory comments and the Bible passage.

Helpful Notes
* *The king's edict.* Pharaoh initially ordered the Hebrew midwives to kill all male Israelite children at birth. Being God-fearing women, they found a creative excuse to let the boys live (see Ex. 1:19). Pharaoh then decreed that all newborn males be thrown into the Nile.

Refer to Helpful Notes when they pertain to your discussion. A group member may read them aloud.

1. Moses' parents saw that he was "no ordinary child." What do think this means?

2. Imagine being Moses' parents. What risks did they take? How were these risks connected to their faith in God?

For question I, have someone read Exodus 2:2 and Acts 7:20. The cross-references are interesting, though they don't spell out precisely what "no ordinary child" means.

Read Hebrews 11:24-26. Raised as the son of Pharaoh's daughter in the splendor of the Egyptian palace, young Moses seems to be on easy street. But then, against all

When discussing question 2, you may want someone to read the story of Moses' birth (Ex. 2:1-10).

odds, he decides to take the road of hardship and sacrifice.

> *[24]By faith Moses, when he had grown up, refused to be known as the son of Pharaoh's daughter. [25]He chose to be mistreated along with the people of God rather than to enjoy the pleasures of sin for a short time. [26]He regarded disgrace for the sake of Christ as of greater value than the treasures of Egypt, because he was looking ahead to his reward.*

Helpful Notes

- *Disgrace for the sake of Christ.* While it's debatable how much, if anything, Moses knew about Christ, he deliberately throws his lot in with God's people and therefore with God himself. And he looks forward to God's salvation, which finally culminates in Jesus Christ. The allusion to Christ serves as a concrete tie-in with the audience of Hebrews; they too must learn that faith in Jesus can and does bring us sacrifice and hardship in the short run, and "our reward" only in the long run.
- *Treasures of Egypt.* The treasures of the tomb of Tutankhamen, who lived around a hundred years after Moses, contained thousands of pounds of pure gold. Moses also had access to this great wealth.

1. What choices does Moses make? What are the consequences?

2. How does Moses demonstrate the definition of faith from Hebrews 11:1?

Leader: A more personal version of question 3: Is there any way in which your faith walk is a wilderness experience?

3. In what ways, if any, does our society make our faith in Christ easy and rewarding? In what ways, if any, does it make our faith difficult and sacrificial? In which direction does the balance tip?

Read Hebrews 11:27-28. Moses' faith causes him to obey an invisible God rather than Pharaoh, even if that action takes him into the wilderness.

> *[27]By faith he left Egypt, not fearing the king's anger; he persevered because he saw him who is invisible. [28]By faith he kept the Passover and the sprinkling of blood, so that the destroyer of the firstborn would not touch the firstborn of Israel.*

1. Like his parents, Moses does not fear the king's anger. Does faith banish all fear? If not, what does this phrase mean?

2. Celebrating the Passover is a strange and new symbol from God. Why does it take faith to keep the Passover and to sprinkle the blood?

Leader: You may want to read Exodus 2:14 in connection with question 1. Exodus 12 (question 2) describes the Passover in detail.

Read Hebrews 11:29 and Exodus 14:10-11, 13, 21-31.
No single story defines ancient Israel more than the dramatic exodus from Egypt. It is this great event that God has been preparing Moses to lead.

> *²⁹By faith the people passed through the Red Sea as on dry land; but when the Egyptians tried to do so, they were drowned.*
>
> *—Hebrews 11:29*

> *¹⁰As Pharaoh approached, the Israelites looked up, and there were the Egyptians, marching after them. They were terrified and cried out to the LORD. ¹¹They said to Moses, "Was it because there were no graves in Egypt that you brought us to the desert to die?". . .*

> *¹³Moses answered the people, "Do not be afraid. Stand firm and you will see the deliverance the LORD will bring you today." . . .*

> *²¹Then Moses stretched out his hand over the sea, and all that night the LORD drove the sea back with a strong east wind and turned it into dry land. The waters were divided, ²²and the Israelites went through the sea on dry ground, with a wall of water on their right and on their left.*

> *²³The Egyptians pursued them, and all Pharaoh's horses and chariots and horsemen followed them into the sea. ²⁴In the morning watch of the night the LORD looked down from the pillar of fire and cloud at the Egyptian army and threw it into confusion. . . .*

> *²⁶Then the LORD said to Moses, "Stretch out your hand over the sea so that the waters may flow back over the Egyptians and their chariots and horsemen." ²⁷Moses stretched out his hand over the sea, and at daybreak the sea went back to its place. The Egyptians were fleeing toward it, and the LORD swept them into the sea ²⁸ . . . Not one of them survived.*

> *²⁹But the Israelites went through the sea on dry ground, with a wall of water on their right and on*

The exodus story begs to be read dramatically, with a sense of wonder and awe at the mighty power of the Lord. Perhaps you can ask a group member to look it over prior to your meeting, then read it to the group.

*their left. ³⁰That day the L*ORD *saved Israel from the hands of the Egyptians, and Israel saw the Egyptians lying dead on the shore. ³¹And when the Israelites saw the great power the L*ORD *displayed against the Egyptians, the people feared the L*ORD *and put their trust in him and in Moses his servant.*

—from Exodus 14

1. Think about the behavior of God's people as described in Exodus 14. If you had been writing Hebrews, would you have included them in your list of heroes of faith? Why or why not?

2. How would this passage have encouraged the persecuted Christians whom Hebrews addresses? Does it encourage you?

Leader: Ask someone to read Main Ideas and Good News. Give the group an opportunity to react to the statements and to add any statements they feel are needed.

MAIN IDEAS

• Our faith looks beyond the immediate and allows us to make choices that honor God.

• Acting on our faith can cause us to make choices that put us at risk and that bring sacrifice and hardships.

• God comes through for those who believe in him. Our acts of faith will be rewarded.

GOOD NEWS

"Do not be afraid. Stand firm and you will see the deliverance the LORD will bring you today" (Ex. 14:13).

REFLECTION TIME

7-10 minutes

You might ask your group if this time of individual reflection is working for them. Does it need to be modified in some way?

Jot down your personal reflections, using the questions below.

1. In what ways has God "come through" for me? How can I thank and praise God for these things?

2. Have my faith choices cost me anything? Am I willing to ask God to prepare me to make difficult faith choices, even if those choices bring sacrifice and hardship? How can the group pray for me today?

3. Is there someone I know who is facing a difficult choice? If so, can the group pray for that person today or during the week?

PRAYER TIME

PREPARATION

5-10 minutes

Share, as you are comfortable, any insight you received in your reflection time. Share especially insights that will help the group pray meaningfully with you and for you.

PRAYER

10-15 minutes

- Begin with this responsive reading of praise from the song of Moses and Miriam (from Exodus 15):

Leader
I will sing to the LORD
    for he is highly exalted.
The horse and its rider
    he has hurled into the sea.

Group
The LORD is my strength and my song;
    he has become my salvation.
He is my God, and I will praise him,
    my father's God, and I will exalt him.

Leader: Go around the circle, giving each person a chance to share his or her response to one or two of the reflection questions. Encourage members to mention ways that you as a group can pray for them.

Ask someone to read these guidelines aloud before the prayer time begins, so that everyone knows the format.

The song of Miriam and Moses is set to music in "I Will Sing unto the LORD" (*Psalter Hymnal,* 152).

43

Leader

The LORD is a warrior;
the LORD is his name.
Pharaoh's chariots and his army
he has hurled into the sea.

Group

Your right hand, O LORD,
was majestic in power.
In the greatness of your majesty,
you threw down those who opposed you.

Leader

Who among the gods is like you, O LORD?
Who is like you—
majestic in holiness,
awesome in glory,
working wonders?

Group

In your unfailing love you will lead
the people you have redeemed.
In your strength you will guide them
to your holy dwelling.

All

The LORD will reign
for ever and ever.
Sing to the LORD,
for he is highly exalted.

- After the reading, group members may offer their own praise and thanks for the things God has done for them.

- Continue your prayer time with items mentioned during the reflection time.

- Ask someone to close your prayer by reading Habakkuk 3:2, 17-19 (or recite it together).

Leader: If you haven't already done so, you may want to talk about a group service project. What could the group do that would match the interests, gifts, and resources of group members? When could you do this? Who will take the lead?

PLANNING FOR MINISTRY

Session 3 suggested that the group as a whole or individual members undertake a "venture of faith." Return to that idea today. Is this appropriate for your group? Has any progress been made? Have individual members committed themselves to a faith venture of some kind?

BY FAITH, RAHAB

OPENING SHARE TIME

10-15 minutes

Next in Hebrews' impressive list of people of faith is a surprise—an "outsider," a prostitute named Rahab.

1. What does it mean to be an outsider? Who would you consider to be "outsiders" in our society today?

2. Share with the group a time in your own life when you felt like an outsider.

BIBLE DISCOVERY TIME

20-30 minutes

Read Joshua 2. Joshua has just replaced Moses as the leader of God's people. It's a time to be "strong and courageous," for the people must cross the Jordan and conquer the fierce and wicked Canaanites, including those living in the ancient and well-fortified city of Jericho.

¹Then Joshua son of Nun secretly sent two spies from Shittim. "Go, look over the land," he said, "especially Jericho." So they went and entered the house of a prostitute named Rahab and stayed there.

²The king of Jericho was told, "Look! Some of the Israelites have come here tonight to spy out the land." ³So the king of Jericho sent this message to Rahab: "Bring out the men who came to you and entered your house, because they have come to spy out the whole land."

⁴But the woman had taken the two men and hidden them. She said, "Yes, the men came to me, but I did not know where they had come from. ⁵At dusk, when it was time to close the city gate, the men left. I don't know which way they went. Go after them quickly. You may catch up with them." ⁶(But she had taken them up to the roof and hidden them under the stalks of flax she had laid out on the roof.) ⁷So the men set out in pursuit of the spies on the road that leads to the

Leader: Before you begin this session, you may want to use a marker to highlight questions throughout the session that seem to best fit the group. This will help you budget your time. Occasionally, you may want to substitute your own questions for the ones suggested in this book.

Try using the "reader's theater" format for the story of Rahab. You'll need readers for the following characters: Joshua, newsbearer to the king; the king of Jericho; and Rahab. Use one reader for the lines of the men (spies). A narrator can read the lines that are not in quotation marks.

fords of the Jordan, and as soon as the pursuers had gone out, the gate was shut.

[8]Before the spies lay down for the night, she went up on the roof [9]and said to them, "I know that the LORD has given this land to you and that a great fear of you has fallen on us, so that all who live in this country are melting in fear because of you. [10]We have heard how the LORD dried up the water of the Red Sea for you when you came out of Egypt, and what you did to Sihon and Og, the two kings of the Amorites east of the Jordan, whom you completely destroyed. [11]When we heard of it, our hearts melted and everyone's courage failed because of you, for the LORD your God is God in heaven above and on the earth below. [12]Now then, please swear to me by the LORD that you will show kindness to my family, because I have shown kindness to you. Give me a sure sign [13]that you will spare the lives of my father and mother, my brothers and sisters, and all who belong to them, and that you will save us from death."

[14]"Our lives for your lives!" the men assured her. "If you don't tell what we are doing, we will treat you kindly and faithfully when the LORD gives us the land."

[15]So she let them down by a rope through the window, for the house she lived in was part of the city wall. [16]Now she had said to them, "Go to the hills so the pursuers will not find you. Hide yourselves there three days until they return, and then go on your way."

[17]The men said to her, "This oath you made us swear will not be binding on us [18]unless, when we enter the land, you have tied this scarlet cord in the window through which you let us down, and unless you have brought your father and mother, your brothers and all your family into your house. [19]If anyone goes outside your house into the street, his blood will be on his own head; we will not be responsible. As for anyone who is in the house with you, his blood will be on our head if a hand is laid on him. [20]But if you tell what we are doing, we will be released from the oath you made us swear."

[21]"Agreed," she replied. "Let it be as you say." So she sent them away and they departed. And she tied the scarlet cord in the window.

²²When they left, they went into the hills and stayed there three days, until the pursuers had searched all along the road and returned without finding them. ²³Then the two men started back. They went down out of the hills, forded the river and came to Joshua son of Nun and told him everything that had happened to them. ²⁴They said to Joshua, "The LORD has surely given the whole land into our hands; all the people are melting in fear because of us."

Helpful Notes

- *A prostitute named Rahab.* Some commentators want to make Rahab an innkeeper, a merchant, or some other nice kind of person. We shouldn't try to sanitize Rahab's reputation, because the point is precisely that God will accept anyone who has faith—even a Canaanite prostitute.

- *For the LORD your God is God in heaven above and on the earth below.* For a Canaanite polytheist to confess this is nothing short of amazing. She not only sees Yahweh's power but believes that Yahweh is God of all. Her words are another way of stating the confession that identifies every Israelite as one of God's chosen people: "Hear, O Israel: the LORD our God, the LORD is one" (Deut. 6:4).

- *This scarlet cord.* According to the *NIV Study Bible,* the early church viewed the cord as a type (symbol) of Christ's atonement. However, the text itself does not attach any meaning to the cord other than its being a way for the spies to identify Rahab and keep their oath to her.

1. How is Rahab's belief in God different from that of her fellow Canaanites?

2. Look closely at Rahab's "confession of faith." How does it show her faith in God?

3. How do Rahab's actions show her to be a woman of faith?

Read Joshua 6:20-25. God promises Joshua that Jericho will fall. All Joshua and his army need do is march around the city each day for six days. On the seventh day they must march around it seven times; then the trumpets will blast, all the people will shout, and the massive walls of Jericho will come tumblin' down.

Leader: Refer to Helpful Notes when they pertain to your discussion. A group member may read them aloud.

The *NIV Study Bible* offers an interesting analysis of Rahab's confession (question 2) to which you may want to refer. See its comments on verses 8-11.

Leader: Continue your "reader's theater" for this passage. You will not need any new readers.

[20]*When the trumpets sounded, the people shouted, and at the sound of the trumpet, when the people gave a loud shout, the wall collapsed; so every man charged straight in, and they took the city.* [21]*They devoted the city to the LORD and destroyed with the sword every living thing in it—men and women, young and old, cattle, sheep and donkeys.*

[22]*Joshua said to the two men who had spied out the land, "Go into the prostitute's house and bring her out and all who belong to her, in accordance with your oath to her."* [23]*So the young men who had done the spying went in and brought out Rahab, her father and mother and brothers and all who belonged to her. They brought out her entire family and put them in a place outside the camp of Israel.*

[24]*Then they burned the whole city and everything in it, but they put the silver and gold and the articles of bronze and iron into the treasury of the LORD's house.* [25]*But Joshua spared Rahab the prostitute, with her family and all who belonged to her, because she hid the men Joshua had sent as spies to Jericho—and she lives among the Israelites to this day.*

Helpful Notes

- *Destroyed every living thing.* A harsh judgment brought on by the grossly immoral and perverted practices of the inhabitants. One of these was to put live babies in jars and build the jars into the city walls as a foundation sacrifice. The land needed a thorough cleansing so the wickedness of the inhabitants would not defile Israel's service of Yahweh. That's why their action is called "devoting" the city to the Lord.

1. Imagine Rahab and her family waiting in her house for the Israelites to attack. The city was "tightly shut up because of the Israelites. No one went out and no one came in" (6:1). There was nothing to do but wait. What might she have been thinking? Feeling?

2. Compare Joshua 2:15 and Joshua 6:20, 22. What miracle is apparent in regard to Rahab's house? What does this say to us about God?

3. Does it seem fair to you that, of all the people in Jericho, a prostitute and her family were the only ones spared? What is God telling us through this story?

Read Hebrews 11:30-31. This is how the writer of Hebrews sums up the story we've just read.

> *[30]By faith the walls of Jericho fell, after the people had marched around them for seven days.*
>
> *[31]By faith the prostitute Rahab, because she welcomed the spies, was not killed with those who were disobedient.*

1. Reflect together on how the conquest of Jericho took faith. Faith on whose part? In what?

2. Why does the writer of Hebrews deliberately mention Rahab's unsavory past?

Leader: You might mention that James also says that Rahab was a prostitute (James 2:25).

3. Verse 31 reminds us that the prostitute Rahab "was not killed with those who were disobedient." But hold on! Didn't she sell out her own people? Didn't she cut a deal to save her own skin? Didn't she deliberately lie instead of trusting God to handle the situation? Aren't these acts of disobedience? Comment.

4. By faith what did Rahab see that the people of Jericho did not see?

MAIN IDEAS

- Simply recognizing God's great power will not save us, nor will an acknowledgment of the great works God has done.

- Only true faith—shown in commitment and obedience—leads to salvation.

- Our acceptance by God does not depend on who we are, where we've come from, or what we've done. God's mercy is open to all.

- God is faithful to all of his promises.

There are many faith lessons in today's Scripture. If time permits, ask group members to give their ideas before reading Main Ideas and Good News.

GOOD NEWS

"For God so loved the world that he gave his one and only Son, that *whosoever* [italics ours] believes in him shall not perish but have eternal life" (John 3:16).

REFLECTION TIME

7-10 minutes

Leader: Group members work individually during this time. Jot down your own personal responses to reflection questions.

Jot down your personal reflections, using the questions below.

1. God accepts me "just as I am." Jot down a sentence of praise for this great news.

2. Do I model Christ's open acceptance of all who believe in him? Do I need to ask forgiveness for sometimes not doing so?

3. Is who I am, where I've come from, what I've done . . . in any way holding me back in my relationship with God? If so, can the group pray that I will know the comfort and joy of feeling fully assured of my salvation in Christ?

4. Is there someone who needs to hear (from me) the good news of acceptance in Christ? Can the group pray for that person today?

PRAYER TIME

PREPARATION
5-10 minutes

Share, as you are comfortable, any insight you received in your reflection time. Mention other prayer concerns that you have as well.

PRAYER
10-15 minutes

- Begin by singing (or reading) the old hymn, "Just As I Am, Without One Plea."

    Just as I am, without one plea
    but that thy blood was shed for me,
    and that thou bidd'st me come to thee,
    O Lamb of God, I come, I come.

    Just as I am, and waiting not
    to rid my soul of one dark blot,
    to thee, whose blood can cleanse each spot,
    O Lamb of God, I come, I come.

    Just as I am, though tossed about
    with many a conflict, many a doubt,
    fightings and fears within without,
    O Lamb of God, I come, I come.

    Just as I am, thou wilt receive,
    wilt welcome, pardon, cleanse, relieve,
    because thy promise I believe,
    O Lamb of God, I come, I come.
    —*Charlotte Elliott, 1836*

- After the song or reading, have a minute or so of silence during which group members can bring matters of confession or personal concern to God.

- Continue in prayer by remembering the requests that were mentioned earlier. Remember especially to intercede for persons who may feel they are on the fringes of the church.

- Ask someone to close your prayer by reading the last stanza of "Just As I Am" aloud.

Leader: Go around the circle, giving each person a chance to share his or her response to one or two of the reflection questions. Encourage members to mention ways in which you as a group can pray for them.

Ask someone to read these guidelines aloud before the prayer time begins so that everyone will know the format.

PLANNING FOR MINISTRY

Leader: The good news of acceptance in Christ suggests some clear directions for ministry. For instance, is the group open to expansion or spinning off a new group? Have any steps been taken to invite a new person to the group? Does the group use the "empty chair strategy" described in session 2?

On a personal level, group members can pray this week for someone who they sense may feel "outside" the fellowship of the congregation. A simple act of service or kindness to such an individual could make our prayers more meaningful.

Session 7

THE GREAT CLOUD OF WITNESSES

OPENING SHARE TIME

10-15 minutes

The writer of Hebrews wraps up his long list of heroes of faith, then encourages us to run the race that's been marked out for us.

1. What characteristics would a coach look for in a long-distance runner?

2. How would you describe your progress in the race of faith? Are you moving right along in good form and discipline? Ready for the hundred-meter dash but not for the marathon? Distracted by the guy selling popcorn? Too tired to even think about it?

Leader: For question 2, encourage the group to be creative and think of more options.

BIBLE DISCOVERY TIME

20-30 minutes

Read Hebrews 11:32-38. This passage starts out with a list of specific people of faith, then lists acts of unnamed heroes of faith. The situations mentioned are varied: some good (33-35), most very difficult (35-38). We need faith on sunny and cloudy days alike, until the great day dawns and our faith becomes sight.

The group may want to identify some of the unnamed heroes of faith in this passage (the *NIV Study Bible* is helpful here), but don't spend too much time with this. Encourage group members to study these people of faith on their own.

³²And what more shall I say? I do not have time to tell about Gideon, Barak, Samson, Jephthah, David, Samuel and the prophets, ³³who through faith conquered kingdoms, administered justice, and gained what was promised; who shut the mouths of lions, ³⁴quenched the fury of the flames, and escaped the edge of the sword; whose weakness was turned to strength; and who became powerful in battle and routed foreign armies. ³⁵Women received back their dead, raised to life again. Others were tortured and refused to be released, so that they might gain a better resurrection. ³⁶Some faced jeers and flogging, while still others were chained and put in prison. ³⁷They were stoned; they were sawed in two; they were put to death by the sword. They went about in sheepskins and goatskins, destitute, persecuted and mistreated—³⁸the world was not worthy of them. They wandered in deserts and mountains, and in caves and holes in the ground.

Helpful Notes

Leader: Refer to Helpful Notes when they pertain to your discussion. A group member may read them aloud.

- *The world was not worthy of them.* These people of faith did nothing to warrant persecution. Their mistreatment was the natural response of a world that has no room for God or God's truth (John 1:10-11). As a result they had to find their home where others had refused to live (v. 38). They were citizens of God's country but aliens in the world.

1. How are the examples of faith alike? How are they different?

2. Why do you think the writer switches from specific people of faith (in most of the chapter) to circumstances that unnamed people of faith endured?

3. What impact would this passage likely have on the original audience of Hebrews? What impact does it have on you?

Read Hebrews 11:39-40. The writer of Hebrews stops to catch his breath and make a couple of observations that apply to all the examples he cited.

> ³⁹*These were all commended for their faith, yet none of them received what had been promised. ⁴⁰God had planned something better for us so that only together with us would they be made perfect.*

Helpful Notes

- *Had planned something better for us.* Not better earthly circumstances but better spiritual conditions ushered in by Jesus Christ. God gives us who live in the New Testament era a better priest who makes a better sacrifice, allowing us more complete access to God (see Hebrews 8).

1. What's the meaning of "None of them received what had been promised"? Doesn't this contradict verse 33, which says that they "gained what was promised"?

2. What's the promise for us today in verse 40?

Read Hebrews 12:1-3. We now come to the all-important "therefore," which signals the "application" of the short sermon we've been hearing. Now, in good

54

preaching style, the writer drives home his point with (of all things!) a reference to the world of sports.

> [1] *Therefore, since we are surrounded by such a great cloud of witnesses, let us throw off everything that hinders and the sin that so easily entangles, and let us run with perseverance the race marked out for us.* [2] *Let us fix our eyes on Jesus, the author and perfecter of our faith, who for the joy set before him endured the cross, scorning its shame, and sat down at the right hand of the throne of God.* [3] *Consider him who endured such opposition from sinful men, so that you will not grow weary and lose heart.*

Helpful Notes

- *Surrounded by a great cloud of witnesses.* The believers of old have already reached the finish line. Now they sit in the bleachers, anxiously watching to see how those still running will do.
- *Throw off everything that hinders.* In those days tunics were tossed aside and races were run in the buff (that's why the stadium was called a "gymnasium," which comes from the Greek word for "naked").

1. What would it mean to the original audience that they were "surrounded by such a great cloud of witnesses"?

2. Use your imagination and picture the bleachers full of saints who are cheering for you. Who's among them? How are they encouraging you?

3. What kinds of things should we "throw off" that might hinder us as we run our race of faith?

4. As you run the race of faith, what does it mean to you to "keep your eyes on Jesus"?

MAIN IDEAS

- We are surrounded by a host of known and unknown witnesses who have finished the race of faith. As we run our own races, these witnesses are cheering us on from the stands.

- Like them, we are called to endure, to persevere, to press on toward the finish line. Unlike them, we have received God's promised Messiah.

Leader: When discussing question 4, look at the qualifications Jesus has to be our model of faith (see Hebrews 12:2-3).

The race metaphor was also a favorite of the apostle Paul. After reading Main Ideas and Good News, you might ask someone to read Philippians 3:12-14 to the group.

- As we run, we need to put away everything that will encumber us or divert our attention. We need to keep our eyes on Jesus, the one who gives us faith and who perfects it.

GOOD NEWS

"God had planned something better for us" (Heb. 11:40).

REFLECTION TIME

7-10 minutes

Leader: Group members work individually during this time. Jot down your own responses to the reflection questions.

Jot down your own reflections, using the questions below.

1. There's certainly a great deal in today's Scripture for which we should thank and praise God. One thing that encourages me, that moves me to praise the Lord is . . .

2. One hindrance or distraction that I would like God to help me deal with is . . .

3. Someone I know who needs encouragement in his or her spiritual race is . . .

4. Today, I would like the group to pray for . . .

PRAYER TIME

PREPARATION

5-10 minutes

Share, as you are comfortable, any insight you received in your reflection time. Mention other prayer concerns that you have as well.

PRAYER

10-15 minutes

- Begin with prayers of thanks, as expressed in the statements we just wrote. Give thanks especially for Jesus Christ, the author and perfecter of our faith.

- Have a minute or so of silence during which group members can bring matters of confession or personal concern to God.

- Continue in prayer by remembering the requests that were mentioned earlier.

- Close your prayer by reading these words from Habakkuk 3 in unison:

> *LORD, I have heard of your fame;*
> *I stand in awe of your deeds, O LORD.*
> *Renew them in our day,*
> *in our time make them known;*
> *in wrath remember mercy. . . .*
> *I will rejoice in the LORD,*
> *I will be joyful in God my Savior.*

Leader: Go around the circle, giving each person a chance to share his or her response to one or two of the reflection questions. Encourage members to mention ways in which you as a group can pray for them.

Ask someone to read these guidelines aloud before the prayer time begins so that everyone knows the format.

PLANNING FOR MINISTRY

Today is a good time to review progress on any group goals you made at the beginning of this course.

Please take a few minutes to evaluate your use of the *Acts 2* materials. Here are a few questions to consider as a group: Is the opening share time effective? Do the Bible discovery questions produce good discussion? Has the reflection and prayer time become a meaningful part of your meetings? Are you spending enough time in prayer as a group? Has planning for ministry become part of your group process?

We encourage you to send your reactions to this material to

Acts 2\Sight Unseen
CRC Publications
2850 Kalamazoo Ave. SE
Grand Rapids, MI 49560

Thank you.

Decide what you're going to study next. Are any changes in the location, schedule, or format of meetings needed?

The beginning of a new study is an excellent time to invite others to your group. You might also consider sponsoring a social event to which potential new members could be invited.

APPENDIX A

GROUP GOALS PLANNING SHEET

1. We plan for our group to grow and to spawn a new group by _____
   _____.

   How are we doing?

2. We plan to have an empty chair at every meeting and to pray for a person(s) to come
   and fill that chair. _____yes _____no

   How are we doing?

3. We plan to pray three or four times a week for each of the _____ unchurched persons we have identified.

   How are we doing?

4. We plan to invite, on an average, _____ new people each month.

   How are we doing?

5. We plan to sponsor _____ social events this year.

   How are we doing?

6. We plan to do _____ service projects this year.

   How are we doing?

7. Additional group goals:

   Special joys:

   Problem areas:

Other titles in the Acts 2 Series:

Spiritual Aerobics

Building the Body

Caring Connections

Lightening the Load

Faith On-line